THE LIVING MERKABAH

David Daniel Ahearn

Copyright © 2023 David Daniel Ahearn

All rights reserved.

ISBN: 9798397562904
ISBN-13:

This book is dedicated to all the Teachers who have come before…

Introduction

The Living Merkabah

Within all of us lies a living Merkabah Field. This is an energy field that comprises the Akashic Record of all of the lives we have lived and within it the lessons we have learned and the karma that we are destined to balance.

Melded within this field lies the energy of our Guides, the Angels, the Masters, the Ascended Masters, the Keepers of the Akashic Journal, the Council of Elders and overseeing the macro grid of the Universe, THE SOURCE OF ALL LOVE.

A Merkabah Field is a layered field of energy starting at the middle of the body located near the solar plexus of all human beings. The genesis of all personal experiences, feelings and intentions begins at this point of the field and then expands outward to each layer of the field. Depending on the strength of the navel, this determines the expansion of the magnetic field in all human beings. Because of this, yogic philosophies such as Kundalini Yogi strengthen the navel point through postures, breathing and meditation. These kriyas allow the practitioner to expand the magnetic field through devoted daily practice which is known as Sadhana.

It is of crucial importance to focus the attention on the navel point to maximize the potential of the Merkabah Field. When the practitioner directs a one-pointed focus on the navel point all possibilities become activated and the possibility exists for a Divine Union with the Universal Consciousness.

This union activates the interior Guide structure from the spirit realm and once activated communication with the Guides, Angels and Masters commences and can be accessed at any point throughout the Earth journey. These Guides become an invaluable source of knowledge that can assist the incarnated soul during their journey on Earth.

Some of the Guides are assigned specifically to the individual while the higher vibrational Masters and Angels assist the entirety of the Universe at large. Each of these fields spins either in a clockwise or counterclockwise direction creating a vortex that allows all intentions to be placed within in order for manifestation of all desire to occur.

The Universal Equation to initiate all manifestation is MANIFESTION = INTENTION + BELIEF + ACTION STEP. If these steps are followed it is a Universal Law that the desired manifestation must present itself in the material realm. By placing the intention into the vortex inside the spinning, living Merkabah Field, the intention takes root in the field and then expands outward from the solar plexus into the void of possibility and continues expanding until manifestation occurs. This occurs at the cellular level of the practitioner.

The Living Merkabah Field takes the shape of a star tetrahedron in the center surrounded by the auric and magnetic field of the Yogi that when strong, expands outward towards infinity. Additionally, when balanced each quadrant is associated with a color which illuminates the quadrant giving off a glow from each chakra region in the field.

1

COLOR SEQUENCING:

Within the human body reside 7 chakra systems. These are spinning vortexes that when healthy and aligned ignite the Living Merkabah Field. Each of these chakras has a specific color aligned with the region and affects certain parts of the aspirant's psyche and physical well-being.

RED: This color represents the root chakra whose function is safety, grounding and the right to live. The associating chakra resides near the anus in the human body.

ORANGE: This color represents the sacral chakra which affects the emotions, creativity and sexuality. This chakra is located near the sex organs.

YELLOW: This color represents the solar plexus chakra which affects the will, social self and power. This chakra finds its root near the belly button.

GREEN: This color represents the heart chakra which affects

compassion, love and integration. We know this as the heart chakra.

BLUE: This color represents the throat chakra which affects personal truth, etheric feelings and expression. This color represents personal wisdom. This is known as the throat chakra.

INDIGO: This color represents the third eye chakra that influences extra sensory perception, intuition and inspiration. This chakra is located at the brow point where the pineal gland and third eye is located.

PURPLE: This color represents the crown chakra that aligns with wisdom, transcendence and universality. "Nobility of purpose." This chakra resides at the crown of the head.

Once the Living Merkabah is healthy and each chakra is spinning to its full potential the field becomes alive with the colors of the Guides, Master, Angels and Ascended Masters. Each color ignites in the field a potential for self-realization and for a divine connection with the Universal Grid.

GOLD: This is the color of a healing modality and indicates the ability to heal with the hands with the use of energy. Gold also symbolizes advanced spirituality and discipline and higher knowledge.

BRONZE: Containing similar elements as Gold yet having earthy tones, this color grounds the practitioner in the Earth while allowing for advanced spiritual disciplines. The grounding nature keeps the Merkabah Field aligned with the Earth.

2

PRANA

Prana is the life force of the Divine. Prana is the energy source that fuels the Universe and can be found in fire, ocean waves, the air we breathe, and it is the life force that fuels the personal Living Merkabah Field. When we breathe properly and with intention, we breathe in prana and when we exhale, we release apana. Through meditative breathing we expand our auric field by filling our vessel with the life-giving prana and then contract our auric field with each exhalation.

Like the human body, the Earth and the Universe at large breathes in prana and exhales apana. When the Yogi aligns and synchronizes the breathing to that of the Earth and the Universe, balance is achieved. Because of this, properly breathing and feeding the Living Merkabah Field is crucial for the health and vitality of the field.

The Living Merkabah is a 16-Guide structure with each Guide representing an aspect of the Authentic Self. Each of these Guides, Angels and Masters take a specific role to advance the consciousness of the soul that is experiencing an Earthly incarnation. Each Guide, Angel and Master occupies one of the four quadrants and focuses on enhancing the characteristics of each quadrant.

3

1. INTERIOR DIAMOND (rotates clockwise), personal Guide Structure:

The Interior Diamond of the Merkabah Field (outlined in red) encapsulates the personal and Individual Guides structure. These Guides are unique to the individual and are generally not shared (unless a specific request is made and affirmed) and stay with the Earthly incarnation throughout the entirety of the journey. They make up the interior Guide structure of the personal Merkabah Field and take the form of Knight, Angel, Sage and Guru which is the individual Highest Self.

When perfectly balanced this field begins spinning in a clockwise fashion and light emanates from the center of the diamond radiating outward throughout the entire magnetic field. Each of these quadrants take on specific characteristics to allow the soul to reach its Highest Potential.

1. The Guru (Highest Self) Quadrant, Grounding, Discipline and Devotion:

* * *

The Guru Quadrant, where the Yogi taps into the Highest Self to initiate the whirling of the vortex, is the domain of the conscious practitioner. This energy occupies the lower right quadrant of the square inside the Merkabah Field.

In meditation, we call to our Highest self, the Guru Within, for Guidance which activates the pineal gland and ignites our intuition. We must agree to be consciously aware of our responsibility to elevate ourselves to our highest self. This is accomplished through daily practice of yoga, meditation and physical exercise. By a continued daily devotional practice, ideally in the Amrit Vela (Ambrosia) hours (This occurs from 4-7 a.m.), we take the first step in elevating our consciousness.

Since Earth is a "free will" schooling system, we must take the first step, using our free will, to devote ourselves to our spiritual development. It is not until we take the first action step that our Guide structure is allowed to move into our Field in order to assist us on our journey.

This is essentially dancing the "two-step" with the Universe where we take the first step, and the Universe responds activating the dance.

Activating intention: "I call to my Highest Self, the Guru Within, to lovingly enter my field to activate my Merkabah Field. Thank you for joining me and please allow me to raise my Kundalini Energy and teach me how I may serve."

2. The Knight Quadrant, Strength and Protection:

Generally, this quadrant is occupied by a spiritual presence with an energy that is "the strong silent type." Seldom will we receive direct spiritual guidance from this quadrant, however if we are in need of protection, we can call on this Guide to put a protective shield around our field thereby disallowing any lower vibrational energy from entering the field.

We can identify and label this "Knight" by simply requesting that the energy identify themselves by name. (In my personal case, this Guide is named "Betsy". Rarely, if ever, does Betsy ever directly communicate with me, however if I need protection, I can instantly sense her energy blanketing my field in times of distress.)

This energy occupies the lower left quadrant of the square inside the Merkabah Field.

Activating intention: "I invite into my field my Knight energy to protect me and keep me safe from any lower vibrational energy. Thank you for joining my field and please allow me to raise my Kundalini Energy and teach me how I may serve."

* **NOTE:** Because Earth is a "free will" zone, in our activating intentions we use the word "invite" and avoid using "command". This honors the "free will" of the spirit energy that we are calling.

3. The Angel Quadrant, Love, Joy and Compassion:

The Angel Quadrant is a very light and airy type of energy that resembled that of fairy energy. When the yogi accesses this energy a feeling of joyousness will permeate the personal aura. (In my personal case, this Guide is named Kamala who possesses a very light, airy and joyously energetic feeling. She takes on the energetic feeling of both a mother and a lover)

This energy will often feel like a cheerleader that evokes constant positive energy to lift the spirits of the Yogi. This quadrant will communicate directly using loving energy and the energy is generally light in nature.

This field sits directly above the "Strength and Protection" quadrant to offset the seriousness of the lower quadrant. The "Strength and Protection" quadrant, by contrast, protects the lighter more open and vulnerable nature of the upper left quadrant of the grid.

Both of these fields work together to balance one another, the Angel quadrant lightening the energy of the Strength and Protections Quadrant, while the Strength and Protection Quadrant protects the openness and lightness of the Angel Quadrant.

These create a perfect balance on the left side of the Merkabah Field that radiates outward into the Master's Field that sits right outside of and on top of the interior field of the practitioner.

Activating intention: "I invite into my field Angel energy to bring me love, joy and compassion from the highest energy source. Thank you for joining my field and please allow me to raise my Kundalini Energy and teach me how I may serve."

4. The Sage Quadrant, Wisdom and Knowledge:

Oftentimes this will be the most "vocal" of the four quadrants. Divine Guidance emanates from this quadrant with the wisdom of the Akashic Journal of Knowledge being revealed to the Yogi. In silent meditation, questions can be directed to this upper left quadrant of the living Merkabah Field and answers will be channeled through the Guide overseeing this quadrant (in my personal field this Guide is named Agape and the information contained within this draft has been revealed through the wisdom of Agape.)

The information revealed from this quadrant is unassailable as long as the ego is removed from the process.

Activating intention: "I invite into my field Sage knowledge and wisdom and asked that the Akashic Records be revealed to me to be understood and applied. Thank you for joining my field and please allow me to raise my Kundalini Energy and teach me how I may serve."

4

2. Master/Teacher Field (rotates counterclockwise)

Residing just outside of the Interior Field of energy is the light golden Master/Teacher Energy Field. Gold symbolizes an advanced spiritual life has been attained leaving the gold color bleeding directly into the dark purple Archangel Field.

These are Masters that have lived on the Earth plane and have ascended to a level of mastery in the human body. There are numerous different Masters that could occupy this field in a person's living Merkabah. Masters of all faiths and religious disciplines will move into this field as needed by the practitioner.

This is where a person's personal faith creates the desired Masters to enter this field. Christians may call on the Saints, the Sikhs call on the Gurus or Yogic Masters from the east may fill this energy space.

Four Master Guides generally appear in this field and upon activation the energy spins in a counterclockwise fashion rotating counter to the interior diamond. This creates the beginning of the vortex. Once these Guides are called into action this activates the vortex to manifest whatever intentions we place before the Masters. It is vital to state the intention and then allow the Masters to co-create to formalize the manifestation.

In my personal field the Sikh Guru's reside here along with Anandamayi Ma. I call in the subtle body of Anandamayi Ma and I offer my personal thanks for bringing her feminine sagely energy in to teach me love, compassion and kindness and to remind me that "Whatever will be will be."

In addition to Anandamayi Ma, I give thanks to the entire Golden Chain of Teachers which include Guru Nanak, Guru Ram Das and Guru Gobind Singh. The Golden Chain of Teachers are all of the teachers of Kundalini Yoga who have passed their practice down to their students who therein teach the practice creating a "chain" or lineage of the teachings to last through eternity called The Golden Chain of Teachers. Each Master passes the knowledge on to the next Master which links student and teachers throughout the ages.

THE GOLDEN CHAIN:

1. **Guru Nanak**
    2. **Guru Ram Das**
    3. **Guru Gobind Singh**
    4. **Anandamayi Ma**

Activating intention: "I would like to welcome in the entire Golden Chain of Teachers which includes Guru Nanak, Guru Ram Das, Guru Gobind Singh and Anandamayi Ma into my field. Thank you for being with me and please allow me to raise my Kundalini Energy and teach me how I may serve."

3. Archangels (rotates clockwise)

The Archangels occupy a vibrational light ray different from the others because these entities have not incarnated on the Earth. These are the Guardians of the Spiritual Realm and are there to advance the consciousness of the planet. The dark purple color of this field symbolizes the "nobility of purpose" that the Archangels possess. The Archangels are in service to the elevation of mankind and generally remain in the background working in service of the Yogi and enter into the field only when called.

This field lies outside the field of the Masters that create protection for both the Masters and the individual Merkabah Field. These measures are put in place to restrict any lower vibrational energy from entering the field. As the field continues to expand outward the color variation begins to glow a luminescent gold, then turning a very dark purple sealing the field with a "nobility of purpose."

The Archangels create the shield that protects the entire entity and allows manifestation to occur undeterred.

This field lies outside of the quadrants of the individual diamond of the Merkabah Field. This field occupies the vibrational field of the Universe and merges with the field of the outlying Ascended Masters. When activated this expands the magnetic field of the individual creating a beacon of light from which all manifestation can occur.

3. Archangels (rotates clockwise)

The Archangels occupy a vibrational light ray different from the others because these entities have not incarnated on the Earth. These are the Guardians of the Spiritual Realm and are there to advance the consciousness of the planet. The dark purple color of this field symbolizes the "nobility of purpose" that the Archangels possess. The Archangels are in service to the elevation of mankind and generally remain in the background working in service of the Yogi and enter into the field only when called.

This field lies outside the field of the Masters that create protection for both the Masters and the individual Merkabah Field. These measures are put in place to restrict any lower vibrational energy from entering the field. As the field continues to expand outward the color variation begins to glow a luminescent gold, then turning a very dark purple sealing the field with a "nobility of purpose."

The Archangels create the shield that protects the entire entity and allows manifestation to occur undeterred.

This field lies outside of the quadrants of the individual diamond of the Merkabah Field. This field occupies the vibrational field of the Universe and merges with the field of the outlying Ascended Masters. When activated this expands the magnetic field of the individual creating a beacon of light from which all manifestation can occur.

1. Archangel Michael:

Michael provides protection in the upper right section of the magnetic field preventing any lower vibrational energy from entering the field. Michael protects the energy centers where wisdom and knowledge emanate, and he gives strength to the practitioner to remain grounded, disciplined and devotional. Michael balances the Merkabah with Vishnu and the Knight energy to provide strength and protection to the field.

Activating intention: "I welcome into my field Archangel Michael who brings me strength and protection. Thank you for joining me and please assist me in raising my Kundalini Energy and teach me how I may serve."

2. Archangel Gabriel:

Gabriel teaches joy and compassion from this lower right section of the Merkabah Field providing a sense of joy to the Yogi while they are engaging in grounding, discipline and devotion. Joy is the highest vibrational frequency which when balanced elevates the vibrational field of the Merkabah. Gabriel also provides the feeling of "the joy of learning" from the wisdom and knowledge sector of the grid.

* * *

Activating intention: "I welcome into my field Archangel Gabriel who illustrates to me joy and compassion. Thank you for teaching me how to exhibit joy and compassion throughout my day me and please assist me in raising my Kundalini Energy and teach me how I may serve."

3. Archangel Uriel

Uriel is an advanced vibrational teacher that brings wisdom and knowledge in the lower left sector to the power of the strength and protection. Strength without wisdom becomes aggression and Uriel transmutes the desire to use strength in the face of wisdom. Although there are times when strength is necessary, and resistance is sometimes called for, it is only through wisdom and knowledge do we ever apply force and only when absolutely necessary.

Activating intention: "I welcome into my field Archangel Uriel who teaches me both wisdom and knowledge. Thank you for sharing your wisdom and may you forever share your knowledge with me. Thank you for joining me and please assist me in raising my Kundalini Energy and teach me how I may serve."

4. Archangel Raphael

Raphael possesses the healing modality in the upper left section of the Merkabah Field. Raphael is an advanced spiritual healer and can heal any infirmities in the mind, body and spirit. If the auric field has any tears or holes in the field Raphael may be called on to heal and repair the field. Raphael sits opposite the point on the star which points to grounding, discipline and devotion. Raphael supports committed devotional Yogis by healing their field and when called upon channels healing energy through the practitioner in order to heal the infirm.

It is of vital importance for the Yogi's Merkabah Field to be stable and strong so the nervous system must be strengthened by practicing Yogic techniques such as mudra, mantras, asanas and meditations. By coalescing and strengthening the Yogi's energy field we prepare the physical body for spiritual ascension and communion with our Guide Structure.

Activating intention: "I welcome into my field Archangel Raphael and asks that you please heal any infirmities in my mind, body and spirit. Please heal any tears in my auric field and allow me to be a healing channel for all of those that I encounter throughout this day. Thank you for being with me and please assist me in raising my Kundalini Energy and teach me how I may serve."

6

The Ascended Masters (rotates counterclockwise)

The Ascended Masters occupy a rarified vibrational field of mastery. The vibrant golden color of this field expands outward to infinity creating light that illuminates the cosmos. Each of these Ascended Masters has perfected an incarnation on the Earth plane and oversees the development of mankind in specific areas. Although each of these Ascended Masters have balanced all areas of the Earthly incarnation, they hold space on a specific light ray to advance the consciousness of mankind.

Direct contact with the Ascended Masters can and does occur, however usually our interior Guides act as a conduit to these Ascended Masters which hold a seat on the Council of Elders. Through devotional practice a Yogi bridges the vibrational gap between the Earthly realm and the advanced vibrational rays that the Ascended Masters occupy.

Among the Ascended Masters there is no hierarchy. Each possesses a "self-realization" that has reunited the Master with Source Energy thereby becoming a direct link to the Divine. Their son-ship becomes "The Way" that all humans can follow to reunite with the Divinity of the Source in remembrance of Truth. This Truth is that we are all One and each of us plays a part in this cosmic play called "life."

These Ascended Masters reside in the outer reaches of our Living Merkabah Field and when invited and activated act as the direct connection with the Source. The Masters hold a vibrational frequency that allows the limited human mind and body to access pure vibrational loving energy. By holding this space, the Ascended Masters become our direct pipeline to God, and they seal the Merkabah Field and illuminate it with pure loving light.

Once sealed, the Merkabah Field shines and becomes a beacon for other light sources. As light sources expand around the world the light connects creating one Light that illuminates the Earth space.

This is the purpose and the desired result of continued yogic practice and meditation for the aspirant. With continued practice the effects of a strengthened Merkabah Field cannot be underestimated.

VISHNU:

Vishnu's quiet strength contains a power and strength that when activated makes the Living Merkabah Field impenetrable. Vishnu seals the field and watches over the field assuring that only loving vibrational energy may enter while simultaneously casting out and repelling lower, darker vibrational energy.

* * *

Vishnu's mastery over strength and protection clarifies the safety of any energy aligned with the field while offering the knowledge necessary to act only in peace, love and compassion to all that interact with the field.

Vishnu's energy is felt strongly on the left side of the human body, specifically by the left ear. Vishnu aligns with Archangel Michael to magnify the field with protection and strength. In quietude, Vishnu waits to be called.

Activating intention: "I humbly welcome into my field, Vishnu, Lord of Strength and Protection and I ask that you keep me safe from harm and allow only loving vibrational light into my field. Thank you for joining me and please allow me to raise my Kundalini Energy and teach me how I may serve.".

JESUS:

"Open your heart to love," Jesus proclaims and when we do, we activate the vibrational power of joy that is the highest state of consciousness the Yogi can hold. In this state, all manifestation is possible and when invited into the Living Merkabah Field Jesus illuminates the field with light through the power love, joy and compassion.

All healing and manifestation occur in this field as Jesus aligns with Raphael to heal the field with light, love, compassion and joy. Through Jesus' healing modality the field is illuminated with loving light that projects outward to anyone or anything near the field which therein begins a transcendent healing for all of those open to healing.

The power of Jesus supersedes any lower vibrational energy

The Living Merkabah

and by the simple calling of the name "Jesus" instant healing can occur if the Yogic mind is aligned with the vibrational energy of Jesus.

Jesus occupies the top part of the Living Merkabah Filed and the energy is generally felt in the crown chakra (top of the head) and when one pointed focus is directed to the crown and the Third Eye the portal from Jesus opens filling the Yogi with loving, kind and compassionate light.

Activating intention: "I humbly welcome into my field, Jesus, Lord of Joy and Compassion. Please fill my heart with peace, love, compassion and joy and allow me to be a healing agent through your beloved name. Thank you for joining me in my field and please allow me to raise my Kundalini Energy and teach me how I may serve."

KRISHNA:

Krishna is a Divine Portal to the wisdom of the Universe. Krishna is a rare vibrational entity in that this Master serves on not only the Council of Elders but is also the overseer of the Akashic Records. Krishna possesses the entirety of the diary of the Universe and when called upon disseminates all necessary knowledge required to ascend to self-realization.

Call on Krishna for Divine Information by opening the portal of knowledge from Lord Krishna. Krishna generally resides near the right ear of the Yogi and occupies the entire right side of the Living Merkabah Field. When seeking information listen intently in the right ear for the whispers of Lord Krishna.

Activating intention: "I humbly welcome into my field,

Krishna, Lord of Wisdom and Knowledge. Please teach me all that I need to know to become more aligned with the Source of All Love. Thank you for joining me in my field and please allow me to raise my Kundalini Energy and teach me how I may serve."

BUDDHA:

Buddha, through continued grounding, discipline and devotion, eventually mastered both the mind and the body while incarnated on the Earth Realm therefore Buddha resides on the bottom of the Living Merkabah Field watching over the root and sacral chakra areas of the grid.

Buddha assists us by inspiring us to treat the body as a temple and the mind as an instrument to be used as opposed to being run by the mind. Buddha provides support for the necessary discipline to maintain a daily devotional practice.

Because we live in a "free will" plane, daily activation of the Living Merkabah Field is required. Each day the Yogi must activate the grid through acts of devotional yoga, mantra and mudra therefore we call on our highest self, Archangel Raphael and Buddha to light up our field.

Upon tuning out after Sadhana, we thank Buddha last to ground ourselves in the Earth so that we may go on with our day.

Activating intention: "I humbly welcome into my field, Buddha, Lord and Master of Grounding, Discipline and Devotion. Thank you for being with me to guide me through my daily devotional practice and thank you for bringing peace to my mind and heart. Thank you for joining me in my field and please allow me to raise my Kundalini Energy and teach me how I may serve."

7

THE SOURCE OF ALL LOVE:

There can be no more important act during your Sadhana than to giving thanks to God, The Source of All Love, Prime Creator, The Universe or Divine Light. It is through the Source that we are given the Power of Creation and with this power the ability to manifest whatever we desire.

The Source is the larger Universal Living Merkabah Field that aligns directly with our smaller personal field. If one were to see a picture of the two fields, they would see the larger grid hovering over our smaller grid with lights connecting each grid therein creating a light portal between the two.

When this portal is fully open, we achieve a state of self-realization and we achieve unified Oneness with the Source. By giving thanks to the Source, we acknowledge our place in Creation and we celebrate the unification of Light and the return to Oneness.

Once this is achieved, we complete the Circle of Creation and we return to the harmony of the Sound Current and reemerge into the One. Through sound and light, we remember once again that love is Earth's native language.

Activating intention: "I bow before you, Divine Light, and give praise for your presence in my field. I ask that you please allow me to be a servant of your peace, love and compassion and please bring me today whatever is for my greatest good and the greatest good of all. Please allow me to see and remember the godliness in all that I encounter today. Guide me to the Light for I am here as a Servant of the Divine."

8

ACTIVATE THE LIGHT

The commitment to a daily Sadhana (daily devotional practice) cannot be stressed enough. Through yogic postures, mudras and meditations we strengthen the central nervous system to allow for the activation of our Kundalini Energy which ignites the Living Merkabah Field. Once activated and aligned with the Universal Grid, we establish our relationship with the Divine and bring balance to ourselves and to those around us.

As Lightworkers, we invest in ourselves through daily devotional practice and then act as a light source for those around us. In yogic circles this is called holding "space" for those around us. We hold "light" space around us to give evidence to those searching that the possibility of self-realization not only exists but is achievable and attainable.

The Living Merkabah Field is alive and vibrating with the cosmos, however we must take steps to release the field from dormancy. To do so takes one-pointed devotional focus, but once achieved delivers harmony to the practitioner and eventually the entire Universe.

When we share the kaleidoscope of human expression through love, compassion and kindness we redefine living and by doing so we heal the world of our perceived misery and disconnectedness and reunify with the Source of All Love.

Everything is connected. We are all One and our Universal Oneness will lead us back to the remembrance of where we once came, outreaches of the Source of All Love expressing Itself through the beautiful alchemy of the human experience.

Printed in Great Britain
by Amazon